Best *[signature]*
Donna

THE LITTLE
ALASKAN
Halibut
COOKBOOK

FROM MY BOAT
TO YOUR TABLE

LADONNA GUNDERSEN

Photography by
OLE GUNDERSEN

Published
by *LaDonna Rose Publishing*
Book and cover design
by Ole and LaDonna Gundersen
www.ladonnarose.com
www.facebook.com/ladonnarosecooks

Prepress and technical assistance
by Debra Dubac, 𝕿𝖔𝖉𝖉 𝕮𝖔𝖒𝖒𝖚𝖓𝖎𝖈𝖆𝖙𝖎𝖔𝖓𝖘

First printing March, 2017
Second printing January, 2018
ISBN: 978-1-57833-662-3

Distributed by
𝕿𝖔𝖉𝖉 𝕮𝖔𝖒𝖒𝖚𝖓𝖎𝖈𝖆𝖙𝖎𝖔𝖓𝖘
611 E. 12th Ave., Suite 102
Anchorage, Alaska 99501-4603
(907) 274-TODD (8633)
Fax (907) 929-5550
With offices in:
Juneau and Fairbanks, Alaska
sales@toddcom.com
WWW.ALASKABOOKSANDCALENDARS.COM

Printed by Everbest Printing Investment Ltd., Guangzhou, China, through **Alaska Print Brokers**, Anchorage, Alaska.

CONTENTS

LET'S GET STARTED
Here's what we're about, why we wrote this book and the star of the show
6

THE CLASSICS
Familiar favorites from Alaska's
icy, clean waters
15

SIMPLE SUPPERS
Naturally lean,
healthful
and quick to cook
31

ON THE GRILL
Cooking over an open fire
adds succulent flavor
45

HEARTY DISHES
Alaska Halibut is known as
the "steak of seafood" because of its firm,
flaky texture and outstanding flavor
59

SWEET TREATS
A perfect ending to a
splendid day by the sea
77

INDEX
84

Photo Courtesy of
The City of Homer

HOMER •

Halibut Fish

of the

Let's get started!

Adventure. Variety. A taste of the unexpected-these are the things that vacationers the world over dream of when they think of Alaska. And what do these vacationers eat in their dreams? Why tasty new foods, prepared in exciting new ways that are bold, unique and memorable.

We love our Alaskan community, which is a special one made up of fishermen and people who love to be outside. A passion for great food and a great environment drives what we do. Which is how this book came about.

With four cookbooks under our belts, and 30 years of commercial fishing, my husband Ole and I have gathered and researched reams of information about every kind of fish from salmon, to halibut to crab and shrimp. For us, this book was an opportunity to share the most interesting things we've learned about the Wild Alaska Halibut, along with thirty six of our favorite recipes.

Inside, you'll find simple dishes for quick suppers, intriguing recipes for serving guests and hearty main courses for satisfying meals. Most recipes serve four, but any of them can be cut in half or doubled. Although this book focuses on Halibut, there are a few other fish available that can be used as a substitute. Bass, grouper, swordfish, tuna and mahi mahi all work well.

Though this book is mini, it will satisfy some mighty appetites and introduce you to the world of Alaskan cuisine! Whether it's Hazelnut-Crusted Halibut with Apple Salsa, Halibut Chowder or Halibut Burgers these treasured dishes are sure to be loved by all.

The promise I try and keep with my recipes - are simple, no fancy equipment or hard-to-find ingredients and I take pride in the fact that anyone can make them, whether you're a five-star chef or a first timer - all are a delicious addition to a cook's repertoire of recipes.

May these recipes enrich your life and the lives of those you love.

–Ole & LaDonna

CAPE FA

Ketchikan, A

The Star of the Show
Wild Alaska Halibut

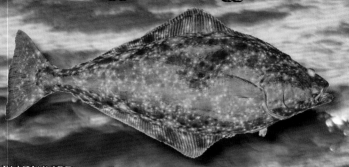

RENOWNED as the world's premium whitefish, Alaska Halibut's mild, slightly sweet flavor and unique, firm texture have made Alaska Halibut a favorite with chefs and consumers alike.

RESPONSIBLY MANAGED
Alaska Halibut is responsibly managed to ensure continued abundance and is strictly regulated through seasonal harvest and the exclusive use of long line gear. Alaska provides the largest supply of domestic Halibut, which is available fresh from March through mid-November and frozen year- round.

WILD
Wild-caught Alaska Halibut mature at a natural pace and swim freely in the pristine waters off of Alaska's rugged 34,000-mile coastline.

SUPERIOR FLAVOR
The superior flavor and texture of Alaska's Halibut is prized around the world. The flavor and color characteristics come from the species feeding on their natural diet of marine organisms and the texture comes from annual migrations in the cold North Pacific.

VERSATILE

It's easy to prepare Alaska Halibut using your favorite cooking method. Whether you like to grill, poach, bake or sauté, you can have a delicious meal on the table in minutes.

HEALTHY

If you are looking for a meal that is nutritious, low in saturated fat and high in the "good fats"- heart-healthy omega-3s, you can start with Alaska Halibut.

ENVIRONMENTALLY RESPONSIBLE

Careful management based on conservation assure abundant stocks of halibut, so Alaska Halibut is an environmentally responsible choice.

ALASKA FAMILIES AND COMMUNITIES

The harvesting and processing of Alaska seafood plays an important role in Alaska. The seafood industry is the state's largest private sector employer. Each fishing vessel is a floating family business, contributing to state and local economies. Alaska's commercial catch accounts for over half of the nation's commercial seafood harvest.

–Courtesy of
Alaska Seafood
Marketing Institute

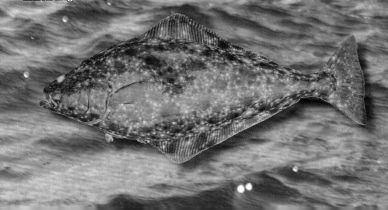

HEALTH BENEFITS OF
WILD ALASKA HALIBUT

Halibut has so many virtues it's hard to know where to start listing them! As a health food, it's superb. It is a first-class protein and low in salt. It contains vitamins, including A, D and B, as well as a whole range of minerals. White fish is low in fat and contains high amounts of polyunsaturated fats called Omega-3 fatty acids. These fats are essential to health because they cannot be produced by the human body and research shows that they reduce cholesterol absorption and help to lower blood cholesterol levels, preventing the arteries from clogging and averting coronary heart diseases.

Omega-3 fatty acids are also believed to help reduce the inflammation associated with arthritis, improve brain function, skin, nails, hair and a well tuned cardiovascular and nervous system.

Fish is perfect for today's lifestyle - it's quick, easy to cook and good to eat!

Whether you are eating fish for the sake of your health or because you love the taste and convenience of it, enjoy the fabulous recipes in this book!

"The fishermen know that the sea is dangerous and the storm terrible, but they have never found these dangers sufficient reason for remaining ashore."
- Vincent Van Gogh

HISTORY OF THE HALIBUT HOOK...

Long before Alaska's commercial halibut fishery existed, long before nylon fishing line, hydraulic winches and fancy "fish finding" GPS systems, Native Alaskans subsisted on halibut.

They fished from dugout canoes with special hooks elaborately carved out of yew wood and fastened together with strands of split spruce root. Fishing line was woven from bull kelp or the inner bark of the cedar tree. And instead of employing a navigating system, they relied on their spirit guides to help them find and catch the mighty fish. Because they fished from small dugout canoes, Alaska Natives had to be careful not to hook a halibut too large - a monster-sized fish would easily capsize their boat.

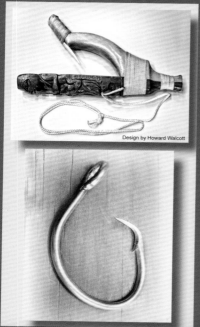

Design by Howard Walcott

For this reason, hooks were designed with just enough space between the base and the barb to catch a halibut no bigger than what the canoe could handle.

The Alaska Natives' clever fishing methods came as a result of quietly studying their prey. Observing that halibut inhale their food (rather than bite or nibble like salmon and other fish do), they designed a V-shaped hook fitted with a barb. When the halibut sucked in the bait, the barb lodged itself in the fish's cheek. Today, commercial longliners and sport fishermen use circle hooks, which are amazingly similar to the traditional Native halibut hook design concept.

In Alaska, you can't wait for the sun to shine or the rain to stop... so just layer up and get out. Soak up the scenery, take a hike, catch a fish, just go. Free the senses and the spirit in the wind, rain, or snow and be inspired by the beautiful scenery.

HALIBUT AND CHIPS

Serves 4

Tartar Sauce

2 cups **mayonnaise**
2 tablespoons **dill pickle relish**
⅓ cup **celery,** minced
⅓ cup **onion,** minced
2 tablespoons **lemon juice**
1 tablespoon **Worcestershire sauce**
pinch ground **mustard**
pinch sea **salt**
pinch ground black **pepper**

Batter

1 cup **Bisquick** mix®
½ cup regular or non alcoholic **beer**
1 **egg**
½ teaspoon sea **salt**

Chips

4 to 5 russet **potatoes,** peel and cut into thin sticks.
  Spread on paper towels. Do not rinse.

vegetable oil (about 4 cups) for deep-frying

1½ pounds **halibut,** skinned, trimmed and cut into pieces,
  each ¾-inch thick

sea **salt** and ground black **pepper**

1 **lemon,** sliced into wedges
4 sprigs of **parsley** for garnish (optional)
ketchup for serving (optional)

Tartar Sauce: In a small bowl, combine all tartar sauce ingredients and mix well. Set aside.

Batter: In a medium bowl, whisk together all batter ingredients until the batter is just combined. If batter is too thick, add additional beer, 1 tablespoon at a time.

Chips: Position a rack in the upper third of the oven and a rack in the lower third of the oven. Preheat your oven to 400°F.

Pour the oil to a depth of 3-inches into a Dutch oven or deep fryer and heat over medium-high heat to 365°. Add the potatoes in batches and fry until they begin to turn golden, about 5 minutes. Using a slotted spoon, transfer to paper towels to drain. In a rimmed baking pan, spread potatoes in a single layer. Bake in the oven until crisp, about 5 minutes. Lower the oven temperature to 200°F.

Fish: Meanwhile, pat the halibut dry with a paper towel and season lightly with salt and pepper. Dip two fillets into the batter, allowing the excess to drip off. Carefully lower them into the oil. Fry, turning occasionally, until golden, about 5 minutes. Transfer the fish to an ovenproof platter and place on the lower oven rack. Repeat to fry remaining fish.

Remove the potatoes and fish from the oven. Sprinkle the potatoes with salt and pile them on the platter with the fish. Garnish with lemon wedges and parsley sprigs.

Serve with the tartar sauce and ketchup if you like.

A Note from LaDonna Rose
For perfectly crisp and golden deep fried food, it is essential to maintain the oil at the correct temperature. Use a deep-frying thermometer and adjust the heat to make sure that the temperature does not fall below 350°, which would cause the food to absorb oil and become greasy.

HALIBUT CEVICHE

Makes **6 cups**

1½ pounds **halibut,** skinned, trimmed and cut into bite-size pieces
¾ cup **lime juice** (about 7 limes)

2 medium **tomatoes,** diced
½ cup **red onion,** finely chopped
½ cup **cilantro,** chopped
2 tablespoons **olive oil**
1 **serrano chili,** finely minced
1 teaspoon sea **salt** or more to taste
⅛ teaspoon ground black **pepper**
½ teaspoon dried **oregano**

mini (3-inch) crisp **tostada shells**
tortilla chips

Put halibut in a glass bowl; cover completely with lime juice. Cover with plastic wrap and refrigerate 1 hour.

Meanwhile, mix remaining ingredients (except tostada and tortilla chips) in another bowl. Chill in the refrigerator while the halibut is finishing.

When the halibut is ready, put into a mesh strainer and strain the fish from the lime juice, put fish into a bowl. Drain most of the juice from the tomato mixture and add to the bowl with the halibut. Gently mix well.

Serve with mini tostada shells or tortilla chips.

A Note From LaDonna Rose
Don't be afraid of frozen fish. While it's not perfect, frozen fish is pretty darn good. Seafood is often flash frozen onboard the ship, or at the very least kept on ice and then frozen right after being trimmed. Much of the fish even at specialty grocery stores has been frozen anyway.

HALIBUT CHOWDER

Serves 4

3 cups **Yukon gold potatoes,** peeled and diced
4 slices quality thick-cut **bacon,** chopped
4 tablespoons **butter**
3 cloves **garlic,** minced
½ cup **onion,** diced
½ cup **red bell pepper,** diced
½ cup **carrots,** grated
½ cup **celery,** diced
½ cup all-purpose **flour**
4 cups organic **chicken broth**
1½ pounds **halibut,** skinned, trimmed and cut into bite-size pieces
2 cups **half-and-half cream**
2 teaspoons fresh **thyme,** chopped
¼ teaspoon ground **sage**
¼ teaspoon sea **salt,** or more to taste
⅛ teaspoon ground black **pepper**
butter pats
fresh **parsley,** minced

Boil potatoes until tender, drain and reserve.

In a soup pot, fry the bacon until crisp. Using a slotted spoon, transfer to paper towels to drain. Add butter to the soup pot; then the garlic, onion, red bell pepper, carrots and celery, sauté over medium heat until soft.

Stir in flour. Pour in the chicken broth. Bring to a slow boil, stirring frequently, until thickened. Add the reserved potatoes, halibut, bacon, seasonings and half-and-half. Gently simmer until the fish is cooked through and the flavors come together.

Ladle into warm soup bowls and garnish with butter pats and parsley.

GRILLED HALIBUT CAESAR SALAD

Serves 4

Croutons
4 (½-inch) thick slices **French bread**, crust removed and cut into ¾-inch cubes
1 tablespoon **olive oil**
2 tablespoons **butter,** melted
3 tablespoons **Parmesan cheese,** grated
2 large cloves **garlic,** minced

Halibut
4 (6-ounce) **halibut fillets,** skinned and trimmed
olive oil for grilling
sea **salt**
freshly ground black **pepper**

Dressing
2 large cloves **garlic**
3 **anchovy fillets**
½ teaspoon **lemon juice**
½ teaspoon Dijon **mustard**
½ teaspoon **Worcestershire** sauce
2 teaspoons **mayonnaise**
⅛ teaspoon sea **salt,** or as needed
¼ teaspoon freshly ground black **pepper**
¼ cup **olive oil**

Salad
1 large head **romaine** lettuce, washed, dried and torn into pieces
½ cup **Parmesan cheese,** grated
freshly ground black **pepper**

Croutons: Preheat your oven to 350°F. In a large bowl combine the olive oil and butter. Stir in Parmesan cheese and garlic. Add bread cubes and toss until coated. Spread the bread in a single layer on a shallow rimmed baking sheet and sprinkle with a little salt. Bake about 15 minutes or until croutons are golden, stirring once. Set aside.

Dressing: In a blender, combine the dressing ingredients until smooth.

Salad: In a large salad bowl, combine lettuce and croutons. Pour dressing over lettuce mixture; toss lightly to coat. Add ¼ cup of the Parmesan and toss well.

Halibut: Preheat an outdoor grill or stove-top grill pan to medium-high heat and lightly oil the grates. Pat the halibut dry with a paper towel and season the fillets lightly with salt and pepper. Grill the fillets until the fish is opaque, flaky and still moist. Turn the fillets over and grill until the fish is just cooked through, about 3 minutes more. **Divide** Caesar salad among four plates and top with a halibut fillet. Garnish with Parmesan and serve.

FISH TACOS WITH MANGO SALSA

Serves 4

Mango Salsa

2 ripe **mangos,** peeled and cut into bite-size pieces
1 cup **red onion,** diced
1 small **jalapeño,** seeded, minced
½ bunch **cilantro,** stems removed, chopped
1 **lime,** juiced
¼ teaspoon sea **salt**
⅛ teaspoon freshly ground black **pepper**

Sriracha Mayonnaise

¾ cup **mayonnaise**
2 teaspoons **Sriracha hot sauce**

12 soft **6-inch tortillas,** heated

1 pound **halibut,** skinned, trimmed and cut into 1 oz. strips
¾ cup all-purpose **flour**
2 eggs, lightly beaten with 2 tablespoons of water
1¼ cups Panko **bread crumbs**
sea **salt** and ground black **pepper**
olive oil, for frying
¼ head **green cabbage,** finely shredded
4 **green onions,** thinly sliced on the bias
2 **limes,** cut into wedges

Mango Salsa: Gently combine all ingredients in a mixing bowl and refrigerate until ready to use.

Sauce: In a small bowl, combine mayonnaise and hot sauce. Refrigerate until ready to use.

Halibut: Pat the halibut dry with a paper towel and season the fillets lightly with salt and pepper. Dredge all the pieces of fish in flour, egg and water, then bread crumbs. Heat a 10-inch skillet over medium-high heat. Add ¼ cup oil. Fry fish in small batches. Drain on paper towels.

To serve, set up the tacos family-style and eat!

BAKED HALIBUT WITH CREAMY PARMESAN TOPPING

Serves 4

4 (6-ounce) **halibut fillets,** skinned and trimmed
sea **salt**
freshly ground black **pepper**

¾ cup **Parmesan cheese,** grated
⅓ cup **butter,** softened
¼ cup **mayonnaise**
3 tablespoons **lemon juice**
4 **green onions,** chopped
¼ teaspoon sea **salt**
¼ teaspoon ground black **pepper**
1 teaspoon dried **dill**
¼ teaspoon **Sriracha hot sauce**

Preheat your oven to 350˚F. Pat the halibut dry with a paper towel.

Line a rimmed baking dish with parchment paper. Arrange the halibut fillets in a single layer in the baking dish. Season the fillets lightly with salt and pepper.

In a mixing bowl combine the Parmesan, butter, mayonnaise, lemon juice, green onions, salt, pepper, dill and hot sauce.

Bake uncovered for 10 minutes. Remove from oven and carefully spread the Parmesan mixture over the halibut and bake for 10 minutes more or until the fish tests done.

BACON-WRAPPED HALIBUT

Serves 4

4 (6-ounce) **halibut fillets,** skinned and trimmed
2 teaspoons **Old Bay Seasoning**
2 teaspoons fresh **dill,** minced
4 slices quality thick-cut **bacon**
4 teaspoons **olive oil**
1 **lemon,** cut into wedges

Pat the halibut dry and season the fillets with Old Bay and dill. Wrap the bacon tightly around the middle of each fillet.

In a large nonstick skillet, heat 1 teaspoon oil over medium-high heat. Add the fish, secured side down and cook turning once until the bacon is crisp, about 8 minutes. Serve immediately with lemon wedges.

A Note from LaDonna Rose
Halibut BLT's are absolutely yummy with this recipe. Or, cut the halibut meat into manageable chunks, then wrap a strip of bacon around the fish and stick it onto a skewer. Put the skewers on the grill. I try to make sure the bacon-covered edge is on the grill so the halibut will not flake. Depending on your grilling style, time will vary, but I cook them until the bacon is cooked.

SIMPLE SUPPERS

POOR MAN'S LOBSTER

Serves **4**

4 (6-ounce) **halibut fillets,** skinned,
    trimmed and cut into equal (3-inch) pieces
8 cups **water**
1 small **lemon,** thinly sliced
¾ cup **sugar**
2 tablespoons sea **salt**
¾ cup **butter,** melted
1 tablespoon fresh **parsley,** chopped

Line a baking sheet with paper towels.

In a large pot over high heat; bring the water, lemon, sugar and salt
to a boil. Simmer for 1 minute. Add the halibut and simmer for 3 to
5 minutes depending on the thickness of the fish.

While the fish is cooking, preheat your broiler to medium-high.

Drain the fish and blot them dry on the baking sheet. Place them in
a 9 x 13-inch shallow baking dish. Brush with the melted butter and
reserve the remaining butter.

Position the baking dish directly under the broiler. Broil the fish
for about 3 minutes until they just start to brown. Garnish with the
parsley. Serve with the reserved warm butter.

A Note from LaDonna Rose
*This easy recipe will amaze you! Hope your family enjoys this
recipe as much as ours does!*

HALIBUT NOODLE BOWL

Serves **4**
1 (8-ounce) package **Asian noodles**
¼ cup low-sodium **soy sauce**
2 tablespoons toasted **sesame oil**
2 cups organic **chicken broth**
4 (4-ounce) **halibut fillets,** skinned and trimmed
sea **salt** and freshly ground black **pepper**
2 tablespoons **olive oil**
2 large cloves **garlic,** minced
1 tablespoon fresh **ginger,** minced
4 **baby bok choy** (about 1 pound), leaves separated
4 **green onions,** trimmed and sliced

Cook noodles according to package directions. Drain and divide among 4 bowls.

Combine soy sauce, sesame oil and broth and set aside.

Pat the halibut dry and season the fillets lightly with salt and pepper.

Heat a large nonstick skillet over medium-high heat. Add 1 tablespoon oil. When hot, add halibut and cook, turning once, until opaque but still moist, about 8 minutes total. Remove and set aside.

Add remaining 1 tablespoon oil to the same pan over medium-high heat. Cook garlic and ginger until fragrant. Add bok choy and cook until wilted, 5 minutes. Add reserved broth mixture and cook until hot, about 4 minutes.

Spoon mixture over noodles, top with a halibut fillet and sprinkle with green onions.

A Note from LaDonna Rose
This is a simple recipe, but in today's busy world, simple is good. Right?

HALIBUT IN PARCHMENT

Serves **4**
2 medium sized **zucchini,** thinly sliced
¼ cup **garlic,** thinly sliced
¼ cup fresh **basil,** thinly sliced,
   plus more for garnishing
24 **cherry tomatoes,** halved
4 tablespoons **sherry cooking wine**
4 tablespoons **olive oil,** divided
sea **salt** and freshly ground black **pepper**
4 (6-ounce) **halibut fillets,** skinned and trimmed

Preheat your oven to 400˚F. Pat the halibut dry with a paper towel.

Cut four pieces of parchment (doubled over) which is large enough to encase your fillet with an inch or so margin around it. I like cutting a heart shape for the packet remember grade school Valentines?

Divide zucchini among one-side of the heart in thin layers. Sprinkle garlic and sliced basil over, dividing equally. Scatter tomato halves around zucchini. Drizzle each packet with 1 tablespoon wine and ½ tablespoon oil. Place a fillet atop each portion. Season with salt and pepper, drizzle ½ tablespoon olive oil over each.

Beginning at the wider part of the Valentine, begin folding the paper over itself. As you move around the paper, you'll end up at the pointed end of the heart, fold under. Place packets in a single layer on a large rimmed baking sheet. Bake until fish is just cooked through (a toothpick poked through the parchment will slide through fish easily) approximately 15 minutes.

To serve, carefully cut open packets (steam will escape). Garnish with basil leaves.

HALIBUT ASIAGO CAKES

Makes **12**
1 tablespoon **olive oil**
½ cup **onion,** diced
½ cup **celery,** diced
¼ cup **red bell pepper,** diced
1 large clove **garlic,** minced
1 pound **halibut,** skinned, trimmed and finely chopped
⅓ cup **mayonnaise**
2 tablespoons **Worcestershire sauce**
½ cup fresh **parsley,** chopped
1 cup Panko **bread crumbs**
¾ cup **Asiago cheese,** grated
¼ teaspoon sea **salt**
⅛ teaspoon ground black **pepper**

Heat a small sauté pan over medium-high heat; add oil. Sauté onion, celery, bell pepper and garlic until soft. Remove from heat to let cool.

In a large bowl, combine halibut, mayonnaise, Worcestershire, parsley, bread crumbs, Asiago, salt and pepper. Add cooled vegetables and combine well. Using your hands and a ⅓ cup measuring cup, form each into a ball. Flatten into thick pancakes. Heat a large sauté pan over medium heat; add a little oil and cook the cakes until golden brown, turning once.

HALIBUT WITH ZA'ATAR AND TOMATOES

Serves **4**
10 large **plum tomatoes**
2 tablespoons **olive oil,** divided
4 large cloves **garlic,** sliced
1 small **onion,** finely diced
1½ tablespoons **za'atar,** (sub thyme)
¼ teaspoon sea **salt**
¼ teaspoon ground black **pepper**
1½ tablespoons **lemon juice**

4 (6-ounce) **halibut fillets,** skinned and trimmed
sea **salt**
freshly ground black **pepper**
20 **asparagus** spears, lightly steamed
1 **lemon,** cut into 4 wedges
½ cup **Parmesan cheese,** finely grated

Slice tomatoes in large pieces. In a large nonstick skillet, heat one tablespoon of the olive oil. Sauté garlic and onion until soft.

Add tomatoes and cook 15 minutes, until soft and chunky. Stir in za'atar, salt, pepper and lemon juice. Cook one minute. Keep warm.

Pat the halibut dry with a paper towel and season the fillets lightly with salt and pepper.

Heat a large nonstick skillet over medium-high heat. Add one tablespoon olive oil. When hot, add halibut and cook, turning once, until opaque but still moist, about 8 minutes total.

To serve, spoon sauce on bottom of four plates. Put fish on top. Serve with asparagus and sprinkle with lemon juice and Parmesan cheese.

SAUTEED HALIBUT WITH FRESH AVOCADO SALSA

Serves **4**

Salsa
2 medium **tomatoes,** seeded and diced
1 **avocado,** pit removed and diced
juice of ½ **lime**
3 **green onions,** sliced
½ cup **kernel corn,** drained
¼ cup fresh **basil** leaves, minced
2 tablespoons **olive oil**
2 cloves **garlic,** minced
1 teaspoon **honey**
¼ teaspoon ground **cumin**
sea **salt** and freshly ground black **pepper**

Halibut
4 (6-ounce) **halibut fillets,** skinned and trimmed
1 tablespoon **butter**
1 tablespoon **olive oil**
sea **salt** and freshly ground black **pepper**
fresh **basil,** minced

Salsa: Gently combine the diced tomatoes and the remaining salsa ingredients in a medium bowl, folding with a wooden spoon to prevent breaking the avocados; season to taste with salt and pepper.

Halibut: Pat the halibut dry with a paper towel and season the fillets lightly with salt and pepper. Heat a large nonstick skillet over medium-high heat. Add the butter and oil. Place the fish in a single layer in the pan. Cook, turning once, until opaque but still moist, about 8 minutes total.

Serve immediately with a generous serving of salsa and a sprinkling of basil.

PARMESAN-CRUSTED HALIBUT

Serves **4**
4 (6-ounce) **halibut fillets,** skinned and trimmed
sea **salt** and freshly ground black **pepper**
¾ cup all-purpose **flour**
2 **eggs,** beaten
1 cup Panko **bread crumbs**
½ cup **Parmesan cheese,** finely grated
2 tablespoons **olive oil,** more as needed

Place flour and eggs in 2 separate dishes; mix bread crumbs and Parmesan in another shallow dish.

Heat a large nonstick skillet over medium-high heat. Add 2 tablespoons oil.

Pat the halibut dry with a paper towel and season the fillets lightly with salt and pepper; dredge in flour, dip in eggs, and coat in panko mixture. Fry flipping once, until golden brown and cooked through.

Serve with your favorite sauce, like tartar or Mae Ploy.

Sustainability Matters
Because we always want there to be plenty of fish in the sea, being informed about the impact your fish has on the environment is important. Ask as many questions as possible: where did it come from? Is it wild or farm-raised? Where does it fall on the Sustainability Index? Larger markets or specialty food stores generally have at least one person on staff who has answers and Monterey Bay's Seafood Watch app is an excellent resource as well. (seafoodwatch.org).

Roasted Halibut Cheeks in Lemon Butter Sauce

Serves **4**
4 to 6 **halibut cheeks**
2 tablespoon **butter,** melted
2 tablespoons **lemon juice**
½ teaspoon **lemon zest**
1 clove **garlic,** minced
¼ teaspoon **paprika**
pinch **cayenne pepper**
1 tablespoon fresh **parsley,** chopped

Preheat your oven to 400°F. In a small bowl, combine butter, lemon juice, lemon zest, garlic, paprika and cayenne.

Pat the halibut cheeks dry with a paper towel and place them in a single layer in a baking dish. Spoon the butter mixture over the halibut cheeks.

Bake uncovered for 8 to 10 minutes or until cheeks are cooked through. Divide between plates, top with pan juices, sprinkle with parsley and serve.

KETCHIKAN WATERFRONT

SEARED HALIBUT WITH MARMALADE GLAZE

Serves **4**

1 **avocado**, pit removed and diced
4 (6-ounce) **halibut fillets,** skinned and trimmed
sea **salt**
freshly ground black **pepper**
1 tablespoon **olive oil**
2 tablespoons **orange marmalade**
1 (8-ounce) can **mandarin oranges,** drained
Hot cooked pearl couscous
⅓ cup **sliced almonds**
¼ cup **dried cranberries**

Pat the halibut dry with a paper towel and season the fillets lightly with salt and pepper.

Heat a large nonstick skillet over medium-high heat. Add oil. When hot, add halibut and cook, turning once, until opaque but still moist, about 8 minutes total. Spread marmalade evenly over each piece of fish.

Mound couscous on dinner plates. Place a piece of fish on top of couscous and arrange avocado and orange segments around the fish. Sprinkle evenly with almonds and cranberries.

HAZELNUT-CRUSTED HALIBUT WITH APPLE SALSA

Serves **4**
Hazelnut Crust
¾ cup dry roasted **hazelnuts**
⅛ teaspoon ground **mustard**
½ teaspoon sea **salt**
¼ teaspoon ground **cayenne**
1 tablespoon grated **lemon zest**
1 teaspoon **thyme** leaves

Fish and Salsa
4 (6-ounce) **halibut fillets,** skinned and trimmed
3 tablespoons **butter,** melted
3 tablespoons **olive oil**
2 tablespoons **green onions,** minced
2 **apples,** cored and cut into ½-inch dice
2 tablespoons **lemon juice**
2 teaspoons Dijon **mustard**
½ teaspoon **thyme** leaves
¼ teaspoon sea **salt**
¼ teaspoon freshly ground black **pepper**
pinch of ground **cayenne**

Preheat your oven to 400˚F. Pat the halibut dry with a paper towel. Line a rimmed baking sheet with parchment paper.

Crust: Whirl ingredients in a mini food processor until nuts are finely chopped. Place nuts on a plate.

Brush halibut with melted butter and pat hazelnut mixture all over. Place on the prepared baking sheet. Bake 15-20 minutes or until fish flakes easily and the tip of a knife inserted into the thickest part shows signs of firming.

Salsa: Warm the oil in a medium sauté pan over medium-low heat. Add onions and apple and cook until slightly softened, about 3-4 minutes. Remove from heat. In a small bowl, whisk together lemon juice and remaining ingredients; stir into apple mixture. Serve halibut with the apple salsa.

BARBECUED HALIBUT WITH SUNDRIED TOMATO-BASIL PESTO

Serves **4**

1 **cedar plank,** soak in water to cover 1 hour; drain
4 (6-ounce) **halibut fillets,** skinned and trimmed
½ teaspoon sea **salt**
¼ teaspoon freshly ground black **pepper**
Sundried Tomato-Basil Pesto

Sundried Tomato-Basil Pesto
¼ cup **dried tomatoes in oil,** drained and minced
2 large cloves **garlic,** minced
¼ cup fresh **basil,** roughly chopped
3 tablespoons **olive oil**
sea **salt,** to taste

Pesto: Place all pesto ingredients in a mini food processor. Process until smooth.

Preheat an outdoor grill or stove-top grill pan to medium-high heat and lightly oil the grates. Pat the halibut dry with a paper towel.

Place halibut fillets on plank; season with salt and pepper. Coat each fillet with the pesto. Place plank on grill rack. Grill fish, 10 to 12 minutes or until opaque.

A Note from LaDonna Rose
What you've heard is true: Fish is more likely to stick than chicken or beef. Your best defense is a grill that's pristine, oiled and hot. That means cleaning it aggressively with a grill brush before and after each use and using a rag dipped in olive oil to thoroughly coat the grill. And remember: as with meat, if the fish doesn't release easily, it's not quite ready to be flipped.

GRILLED HALIBURGERS

Serves **4**

1½ pounds **halibut fillets,** skinned, trimmed and finely chopped
2 tablespoons **onion,** coarsely grated and its juice
2 tablespoons **mayonnaise**
1 teaspoon **lemon juice**
1 teaspoon **Old Bay Seasoning**
¼ teaspoon sea **salt**
⅛ teaspoon freshly ground black **pepper**

Zesty Tartar Sauce
½ cup **mayonnaise**
1 tablespoon **sweet pickle relish**
1 tablespoon **onion,** finely chopped
½ teaspoon dried **dill**
2 teaspoons **lemon juice**
pinch **cayenne** pepper

1 tablespoon **olive oil**
8 slices of brioche or 4 Kaiser **rolls,** split
4 crisp **lettuce** leaves
1 **tomato,** sliced

Patties: In a bowl, combine the chopped halibut, onion and its juice, the 2 tablespoons mayonnaise, lemon juice, Old Bay, salt and pepper. Shape into four firm patties about 1½-inches thick. Cover and chill in freezer for 10 minutes.

Sauce: Combine the ½ cup mayonnaise, sweet relish, onion, dill, lemon juice and cayenne in a small bowl. Set aside.

Preheat a nonstick skillet, outdoor grill or stove-top grill pan over medium-high heat. Add oil to the skillet. Carefully place the halibut patties in the pan with a wide spatula. Cook the patties, gently turning once until golden, about 8 minutes total. At the same time, lightly toast the buns. Slather the bun tops with the sauce. Place the patties on the bun bottoms. Top with the lettuce leaves and tomato slices and enjoy!

GRILLED HALIBUT WITH LEMON BUTTER SAUCE

Serves **4**

<u>**Lemon Butter Sauce**</u>

2 tablespoons fresh **lemon juice**
1 medium **shallot,** finely diced
¾ cup cold **butter,** diced
1 teaspoon **lemon zest**
sea **salt** to taste
chives, chopped for garnish

4 (6-ounce) **halibut fillets,** skinned and trimmed
olive oil
sea **salt** and freshly ground black **pepper**

Lemon Butter Sauce: In a small sauté pan over medium-low heat, add the lemon juice and shallots. Simmer until half the liquid has been reduced. Take the pan off the heat and whisk in several pieces of diced butter. When it's nicely incorporated whisk in a few more pieces of butter. Whisk until the sauce feels smooth.

Place the pan back over medium-low heat and whisk in the remaining butter until the sauce is smooth. Take the sauce off the heat and gently stir in the lemon zest and season to taste with salt. Strain the sauce into a container and ladle over grilled halibut. Garnish with chopped fresh chives.

Halibut: Preheat an outdoor grill or stove-top grill pan to medium-high heat and lightly oil the grates. Pat the halibut dry with a paper towel and rub the fillets with a little olive oil; season with salt and pepper. Grill until lightly charred, 6 to 8 minutes (a bit longer if fillet is thick). Turn and cook until just cooked through (still slightly translucent in the center), a minute or two and the tip of a knife inserted into the thickest part shows signs of firming.

GRILLED HALIBUT KEBOBS

Serves **4**
16 - **Skewers,** soak in water
1½ pounds **halibut,** skinned,
    trimmed and cut into equal chunks
½ teaspoon sea **salt**
¼ teaspoon ground black **pepper**
2 **lemons,** thinly sliced
2 to 3 tablespoons **olive oil**
½ teaspoon dried **oregano**
½ teaspoon dried **coriander**
1 teaspoon **za'atar,** (sub thyme)

Pat halibut dry with a paper towel and place in a medium bowl. Toss with salt and pepper.

Assemble each kebob with two skewers (when you use just one, fish will roll around).

Alternate halibut chunks and lemon, folding the lemon slice in half. Brush both sides with olive oil and then sprinkle with the oregano, coriander and za'atar.

Preheat an outdoor grill or stove-top grill pan to medium-high heat and lightly oil the grates.

Place halibut kebobs on grill and sear on both sides for about 3 to 4 minutes, turning only once. Remove and serve. If using a grill pan, pouring the pan juices over the kebobs is yummy.

A Note from LaDonna Rose
Fish will continue to cook for a minute or two off the heat. Be sure to stop cooking when the fish is just shy of done, otherwise, it will overcook by the time you serve it. Use the tip of a small knife to peek at the interior of the fish. As you peek, see how easily the fish gives way. It should gently resist flaking but show signs of firming. Raw fish has a translucent appearance that turns opaque during cooking.

GRILLED HALIBUT WITH
FRESH STRAWBERRY SALSA

Serves **4**

<u>**Strawberry Salsa**</u>

3 cups fresh **strawberries,** chopped
½ cup **red onion,** finely chopped
1 **jalapeño,** seeded, minced
¼ cup **cilantro,** chopped
2 **limes,** one juiced and zest from one
pinch sea **salt**

4 (6-ounce) **halibut fillets,** skinned and trimmed
2 tablespoons **olive oil**
sea **salt**
freshly ground black **pepper**

Strawberry Salsa: In a large bowl, stir together the strawberries, onion, jalapeño, cilantro, lime juice and zest. Season with a pinch of salt. Let sit 15 minutes.

Preheat an outdoor grill or stove-top grill pan to medium-high heat and lightly oil the grates. Pat the halibut dry with a paper towel and rub the fillets with a little olive oil; season with salt and pepper. Grill over medium-high heat, until lightly charred, 6 to 8 minutes (a bit longer if fillet is thick). Turn and cook until just cooked through (still slightly translucent in the center), a minute or two and the tip of a knife inserted into the thickest part shows signs of firming.

Serve fish immediately with the strawberry salsa.

The Tools You Need...
1. SPATULA You'll want one of those thin, nimble fish spatulas for flipping smaller fillets. Invest in an extra-long grilling spatula that's sturdy enough to slide underneath larger fillets.
2. TONGS Make sure the handle is long enough to keep your hands far from the heat of the grill.
3. AND THE ONE YOU DON'T... Yes, fish baskets are cute, but if your grill is clean enough, oiled enough and hot enough, you don't need one.

GRILLED HALIBUT WITH CITRUS

Serves **4**

¾ cup dry **white wine**
2 tablespoons **molasses**
2 tablespoons fresh **ginger,** peeled and finely minced
4 (6-ounce) **halibut fillets,** skinned and trimmed
2 tablespoons **olive oil**
sea **salt**
freshly ground black **pepper**
1 **lemon,** cut into 4 wedges
1 **orange,** cut into 8 wedges
flat leaf **parsley,** for garnish

Preheat an outdoor grill or stove-top grill pan to medium-high heat and lightly oil the grates.

Whisk together the wine, molasses and ginger in a small bowl. Pour into a shallow baking dish. Lay the halibut fillets in the marinade, turn to coat and let stand at room temperature for 15 minutes.

Drain the halibut, into a small saucepan and pat the fillets dry with a paper towel. Brush with oil and season lightly with salt and pepper.

Boil the reserved marinade for 2 minutes, set aside.

Grill the fillets until browned on the first side 3-4 minutes, depending on thickness. Turn the fish and cook until browned on the second side and opaque throughout, 3-4 minutes.

Meanwhile, place the lemon and orange wedges directly on the grill and cook, turning once until lightly browned on each side. Transfer the fish, lemon and orange wedges to warmed dinner plates. Pour the reserved marinade over the halibut and garnish with parsley.

A Note from LaDonna Rose
Remember: lower the heat rather than raise it and err on the side of under cooking. Fish continues to cook after you remove it from the heat.

GRILLED HALIBUT BURRITOS

Serves **4**
1 pound **halibut fillets,** skinned and trimmed
2 tablespoons **olive oil**
1 teaspoon **chili powder**
½ teaspoon **paprika**
1 tablespoon **lemon juice**
2 tablespoons fresh **parsley**
4 large **flour tortillas**

1½ cups **Cheddar cheese,** grated
lettuce, shredded
cabbage, shredded
red onion, chopped
sour cream
salsa
2 teaspoons **Sriracha hot sauce** mixed with ½ cup **mayonnaise**

Place halibut fillets in a shallow baking dish and coat with olive oil, chili powder, paprika, lemon juice and parsley. Let stand at room temperature for 15 minutes.

Preheat an outdoor grill or stove-top grill pan to medium-high heat and lightly oil the grates.

Place fillets on grill and cook for 6 to 8 minutes (a bit longer if fillet is thick). Remove halibut from the grill and flake, but leave some good size pieces.

Heat tortillas on grill until they are soft and top with fish and preferred toppings and roll up burrito style.

A Note from LaDonna Rose
Frozen fish should be thawed in the refrigerator. The slower fish is thawed, the less it is affected by the freezing process. Never try to speed the process by thawing in the microwave, the texture of the fish will be badly compromised.

Spicy Halibut Burgers

Serves **4**

2 tablespoons light **brown sugar**
1½ teaspoons **chili powder**
1 teaspoon **cumin**
4 (5-ounce) **halibut fillets,** skinned and trimmed
1 tablespoon **olive oil**
2 teaspoons **jalapeños,** canned or fresh, seeded, minced
½ cup **mayonnaise**
4 **hamburger buns,** split and toasted
crisp **lettuce** leaves
sliced **tomatoes**

In a small bowl, stir together jalapeños and mayonnaise. Spread on cut sides of buns. On a plate, stir together the brown sugar, chili powder and cumin. Pat the halibut with a paper towel and press tops of fillets into spice mixture.

Preheat a stove-top grill pan or an oiled skillet over medium-high heat and lightly oil the grates. Add the fillets spice side down, cook 3 to 4 minutes or until browned. Turn and cook another 3 to 4 minutes or until the fish begins to flake.

Place halibut on bottom half of bun, top with lettuce and sliced tomatoes. Cover with top half.

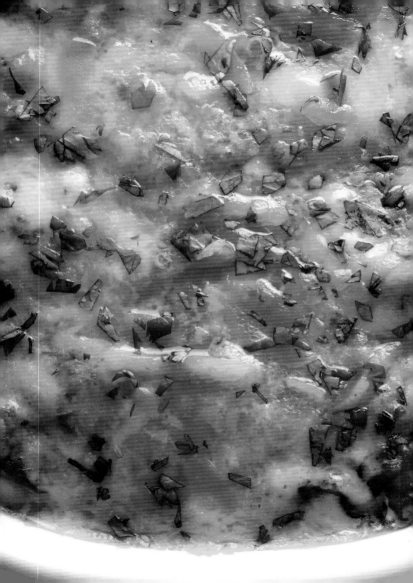

HEARTY DISHES

HALIBUT RISOTTO POMODORO

Serves **4**

4 slices **cooked bacon,** chopped
3 cups organic **chicken broth**
1 tablespoon **olive oil**
¼ cup **red onion,** chopped
3 fresh **sage** leaves, finely snipped
1¼ cups uncooked **arborio rice**
1 cup roma **tomatoes,** seeded and chopped
3 ounces fresh baby **spinach**
1 pound **halibut,** skinned, trimmed and cut into bite-size pieces
1 cup **Parmesan cheese,** freshly grated, divided in half
½ teaspoon sea **salt**

In a medium saucepan over medium heat, bring the broth to a simmer.

Heat the olive oil in a large skillet over medium heat. Add onion and sauté until soft. Add sage and stir for 1 minute. Add rice; cook and stir for 3 to 4 minutes or until rice is lightly browned. Stir in tomatoes.

Slowly add ½ cup of the broth to rice mixture, stirring constantly. Continue to cook and stir over medium heat until liquid is absorbed.

Slowly add 1½ cups more broth, **½ cup at a time,** stirring constantly. Continue to cook and stir until liquid is absorbed. Stir in spinach, then halibut. Add enough of the remaining broth, ½ cup at a time, cooking and stirring just until rice is tender and the halibut is cooked. (This should take about 25 minutes total.)

Gently stir in ½ cup of the Parmesan and season to taste with salt.

To serve, transfer risotto to a serving platter. Sprinkle with remaining Parmesan and bacon.

A Note from LaDonna Rose
This recipe easily doubles!

HALIBUT ENCHILADAS

Serves **4**

1 pound **halibut,** skinned,
    trimmed and cut into bite-sized pieces
¾ cup **cream cheese**
½ cup **sour cream**
4 **green onions,** chopped
2 (4-ounce) cans chopped **green chilies**
½ cup **black olives,** drained and chopped
2 small **jalapeño peppers,** seeded, minced
1½ teaspoons **cumin**
½ teaspoon sea **salt**
10 (8-inch) **flour tortillas**
2 teaspoons all-purpose **flour**
1 cup **half-and-half cream**
½ cup **salsa**
¾ cup **Monterey Jack cheese,** shredded
¾ cup **Cheddar** cheese
⅓ cup **Parmesan cheese,** shredded
¼ cup fresh **cilantro,** chopped

Preheat your oven to 350°F. Coat a 9 x 13-inch baking dish with nonstick cooking spray.

Bring 4 cups of salted water to a boil in a large saucepan. Carefully add the halibut and simmer for 2 minutes. Drain and set aside.

Using a hand mixer, beat the cream cheese and sour cream. Gently add the onions, chilies, olives, jalapeños, cumin and salt. **Gently fold in the fish.**

Place a generous amount down the center of each tortilla; roll up and place in baking dish, Combine flour and half-and-half until smooth; pour over enchiladas.

Cover with foil and bake for 20 minutes or until heated through. Uncover; spread the salsa all over and sprinkle with the cheeses and broil for 1 minute or until lightly browned. Garnish with the cilantro.

BACON WRAPPED HALIBUT BITES

Makes **20**

1 pound **halibut,** skinned, trimmed and finely chopped
1 small **jalapeño,** seeded, minced
3 **green onions,** minced
2 teaspoons **Worcestershire sauce**
⅓ cup **milk**
1 **egg**
1 cup **Cheddar cheese,** shredded
1 cup Panko **bread crumbs**
½ teaspoon sea **salt**
1 pound thin-cut **bacon**
¼ pound **Swiss cheese,** thinly sliced

toothpicks soaked in water for 30 minutes.

Preheat your broiler to medium-high heat. Line a rimmed baking sheet with aluminum foil.

In a large bowl combine, halibut, jalapeño, green onions, Worcestershire sauce, milk, egg, Cheddar cheese, bread crumbs and salt. Using your hands and a ¼ cup measuring cup, form each into a ball. Wrap each ball with bacon and secure with a toothpick and place on the prepared baking sheet.

Broil 12 minutes, turning once, until done. Remove the balls from the oven and place a piece of Swiss cheese on top of each ball. Place back in the oven until the cheese is melted.

A Note from LaDonna Rose
I learned of these fabulous, easy halibut bites from my friend Daniel Kenyon while filming an episode of Ketchikan KPU Celebrity Chef (You can find this episode and many others on YouTube). After the show Daniel became my good friend. Daniel, many thanks for this great recipe!

HALIBUT WITH COCONUT-CURRY AND BOK CHOY

Serves **4**

1 tablespoon **olive oil**
½ cup **shallots,** minced
1 tablespoon Thai red **curry paste**
2 cups organic **chicken broth**
1 (14-ounce) can **coconut milk**
1 teaspoon **sugar**
sea **salt** and freshly ground black **pepper**
½ pound **baby bok choy,** stems trimmed
4 (6-ounce) **halibut fillets,** skinned and trimmed
½ cup fresh **cilantro** leaves, chopped, plus more for garnish
3 **green onions,** thinly sliced, plus green parts for garnish
1 **lime,** half juiced, other half cut into wedges for serving

2 cups **cooked jasmine rice**

Heat a deep sauté pan over medium heat. Add the oil and sauté the shallots until fragrant. Add the curry paste, broth, coconut milk, sugar and ½ teaspoon salt. Bring to a boil; then reduce heat to low and simmer for 8 minutes.

Pat the halibut dry with a paper towel and season the fillets lightly with salt. Gently place the fillets and bok choy into the broth and coat the fish with the sauce. Cover the pan and poach the fillets until almost cooked through, 4-6 minutes (a bit longer if fillet is thick).

Carefully remove bok choy from the pan; place in four soup bowls. Top with the fish.

Stir the cilantro, green onions and the juice of half a lime into the sauce and season, to taste with salt and pepper. Ladle the sauce over the fish. Sprinkle with cilantro and green onion and serve with jasmine rice and lime wedges.

PUFF PASTRY HALIBUT PIE

Serves **4**

6 strips **bacon,** cut into ½ inch dice
1 **onion,** diced
2 cloves **garlic,** minced
3½ cups organic **chicken broth**
3 cups **Yukon gold potatoes,** peeled,
    diced into ¼-inch cubes
½ cup **heavy cream**
1 cup **Gruyére cheese,** shredded
½ cup flat-leaf **parsley,** chopped
pinch of sea **salt**
¼ teaspoon ground black **pepper**
1½ teaspoons **cornstarch**
1 pound **halibut,** skinned, trimmed and cut into bite-size pieces
2 sheets ready made **puff pastry, thawed**
1 **egg,** beaten
a deep round 12-inch **casserole dish**

Fry the bacon, onion and garlic in a large saucepan. Fry until the bacon is cooked through. Add the broth and bring to a boil and simmer for 15 minutes. Add the potatoes and simmer for 10 minutes, then slowly add the heavy cream, cheese and parsley and continue to simmer for another 5 minutes. Add a pinch of salt and pepper to taste.

Stir the cornstarch with a spoonful of the sauce and add it back to the sauce and stir until thickened. Allow the sauce to cool completely. Add the halibut and place in the refrigerator.

Preheat your oven to 350˚F. Roll out one of the pastry sheets on a lightly floured surface and cover the bottom and sides of the casserole dish. Prick the base with a fork and cover with foil and fill with baking beans. Bake in the preheated oven for 10 minutes. Remove from the oven, take out the beans and the foil, then brush the beaten egg all over and bake for 2 minutes. Roll out the remaining pastry. Fill with the mixture, then cover with the pastry. Using the leftover pastry, decorate the top. Glaze with the beaten egg and bake for 45 minutes.

BAKED HALIBUT WITH PISTACHIO-DATE CRUST

Serves **4**

3 tablespoons **butter, melted**
10 **Medjool dates,** pitted
¼ cup **pistachio nuts,** crushed
½ cup Panko **bread crumbs**
4 (6-ounce) **halibut fillets,** skinned and trimmed
sea salt and ground black **pepper**

Place dates in a heat proof glass bowl; add boiling water to cover. Let the dates soften for about 10 minutes. Remove the dates and purée in a mini food processor until smooth.

Stir together date paste, melted butter, nuts and bread crumbs in a mixing bowl and mix well.

Preheat your oven to 350°F. Line a rimmed baking sheet with parchment paper.

Pat the halibut dry with a paper towel and season the fillets lightly with salt and pepper. Press the date mixture evenly into the top of the fillets and gently massage so it sticks. Place on the prepared baking sheet.

Bake for 15 to 20 minutes (a bit longer if fillet is thick) until just cooked through (still slightly translucent in the center) and the tip of a knife inserted into the thickest part shows signs of firming.

Using a spatula, gently turn fish out of the pan and onto serving plates, with breaded side facing up.

A Note from LaDonna Rose
I love this recipe because it's simple and there's not much clean up!

HALIBUT SHEPHERDS PIE

Serves **6**
2 tablespoons **butter**
3 cloves **garlic,** minced
1 cup each **carrots, celery, onion** and **mushrooms,** sliced
¼ cup all-purpose **flour**
½ cup **sherry** wine
2½ cups organic **chicken broth**
1 pound **halibut,** skinned, trimmed and cut into bite-size pieces
1 cup frozen **green peas,** thawed
1 teaspoon dried **thyme**
sea **salt** and ground black **pepper** to taste

Topping
2 pounds Yukon gold **potatoes,** peeled and cubed
4 tablespoons **butter,** cubed and softened
1½ cups white **Cheddar cheese,** shredded
1 **egg,** lightly beaten
1 tablespoon Dijon **mustard**

Preheat your oven to 400°F.

Filling: Melt 2 tablespoons butter in a large, deep oven-proof skillet over medium heat. Add garlic, carrots, celery, onion and mushrooms; sauté until softened. Stir in flour and cook for 1 minute. Add sherry and stir until absorbed. Stir in broth, then halibut, peas and thyme; season with salt and pepper. Bring filling to a boil; then reduce heat to low and simmer for about 10 minutes and remove from heat.

Topping: Cook potatoes in a large pot of boiling salted water until fork-tender. Drain potatoes and return to the pot. Add 4 tablespoons of butter and blend with a hand mixer on low speed until potatoes are smooth. Stir in Cheddar, egg and Dijon; season with salt.

Spoon topping over filling in pan and bake pie until topping is lightly browned, 25 to 30 minutes, let stand 15 minutes before serving.

HALIBUT WITH TARRAGON CREAM SAUCE

Serves **4**

4 (6-ounce) **halibut fillets,** skinned and trimmed
sea **salt** and freshly ground black **pepper**
2 tablespoons **olive oil**
1½ cups **mushrooms,** halve if large
3 ounces **prosciutto,** sliced (if you don't have prosciutto,
   use bacon and drain well or just omit it)
1 cup dry **white wine** or organic chicken broth
1 cup **heavy cream**
2 teaspoons fresh **tarragon**
1 teaspoon **apple cider vinegar**
fresh **chives** or green onions, minced

<u>Rosemary Buttered Noodles</u>
8 ounces **dried egg noodles**
4 tablespoons **butter**
2 teaspoon fresh **rosemary,** minced
Parmesan cheese, grated
freshly ground black **pepper**

Pat the halibut dry with a paper towel and season the fillets lightly
with salt and pepper. Heat a large nonstick skillet over medium-
high heat. Add oil. When hot, add halibut and cook, turning once,
until opaque but still moist, about 4 minutes total. Remove fish, set
aside and keep warm. Add mushrooms and prosciutto to the pan.
Cook until mushrooms soften and begin to brown, 2-3 minutes. Add
wine (or broth) and cream. Return fish to the pan, reduce heat
and simmer until sauce thickens slightly, about 8 minutes. Stir in
tarragon and vinegar; cook 1 minute. Garnish with chives. Serve
with buttered noodles.

Buttered Noodles: Cook noodles as directed on the package.
Drain, but do not rinse. Melt butter over medium heat in the same
pan that was used to cook the noodles. Add the rosemary and
cook until fragrant, about 1 minute. Add drained noodles to the pan
and toss to coat with the butter, then transfer to a serving dish. Top
noodles with Parmesan cheese and black pepper.

HALIBUT AND BRIE IN A PUFF PASTRY

Makes **12**

1 pound **halibut,** skinned, trimmed and diced into
   small bite-sized pieces
1 tablespoon fresh **dill,** finely chopped
¼ teaspoon sea **salt**
2 sheets ready made **puff pastry, thawed**
1 **egg,** beaten
2 teaspoons Dijon **mustard**
1 cup **spinach,** chopped
5 ounces **Brie cheese,** rind removed,
   cut into 12 equal pieces

3½-inch round cookie cutter

Preheat your oven to 375˚F.

Pat the halibut dry with a paper towel.

Line two baking sheets with parchment paper.

In a medium bowl; mix the halibut, dill and salt. Set aside.

Roll out the two pastry sheets on a lightly floured surface to measure
11x11-inches each. You should be able to cut 12 circles from each
sheet using the round cookie cutter.

Glaze the outer edges of the 12 that will be used for the bottoms
with the beaten egg. Spread mustard in the middle of each and
place spinach on top to form a base. Place the halibut on top to
form a mound. Gently stretch the Brie cheese and place over the
halibut. Gently stretch the unused pastry discs then carefully cover
the mounds, sealing the pastry. Using a fork, squeeze the edges
together.

Glaze the pastry with the beaten egg and once the glaze has dried
use a sharp knife to score a pattern on each one. Transfer to the
prepared baking sheets and bake for 20 to 25 minutes.

Braised Halibut Puttanesca

Serves 4

3 tablespoons **olive oil**, divided
4 to 5 large cloves **garlic**, chopped
3 **anchovy fillets**, minced (optional)
½ teaspoon crushed **red pepper flakes**
2 (14-ounce) cans diced **tomatoes**
¼ cup white **cooking wine**
½ cup Kalamata **olives**, pitted and halved
sea **salt**
freshly ground black **pepper**
4 (6-ounce) **halibut fillets**, skinned and trimmed
1 tablespoons fresh **parsley**, finely chopped

Heat a large skillet over medium heat. Add 2 tablespoons of the oil, then the chopped garlic, anchovies and crushed red pepper flakes to the pan. Break up anchovies with the back of a wooden spoon until they melt into the oil. Add tomatoes, wine and olives. Season to taste with salt and pepper.

Season the halibut fillets lightly with salt and gently lay them in the sauce. Cover with a tight-fitting lid. When the sauce boils, reduce heat to low and simmer, 8 to 10 minutes, until the fish is opaque, flaky and still moist. Drizzle remaining tablespoon olive oil over the fish and sprinkle with parsley and serve.

HALIBUT LASAGNA

Serves **6**

12 **lasagna noodles**
3 tablespoons **butter**
1 small **onion,** chopped
5 cloves **garlic,** minced
3 tablespoons all-purpose **flour**
3 cups **half-and-half cream**
1 cup **Ramano cheese,** grated
½ teaspoon sea **salt**
¼ teaspoon ground black **pepper**
dash **cayenne** and **curry** to taste
1½ pounds **halibut,** skinned, trimmed and cut into bite-size pieces
¼ cup **butter** melted
½ cup **Parmesan cheese,** grated
1½ cups Panko **bread crumbs**
parsley and **paprika**

Preheat your oven to 375˚F. **Cook noodles** according to package directions and set aside.

Spray a 9 x 13-inch baking dish with nonstick cooking spray. Melt butter in a large saucepan over medium heat. When butter bubbles, add the onion and garlic, cook until soft. Add the flour. Cook, stirring 1 minute. While whisking, slowly pour in the half-and-half. Whisk until the mixture thickens slightly and coats the back of a spoon. Remove pan from heat. Stir in the Romano, salt, pepper and seasonings to taste. Gently add the halibut.

Spoon ¼ cup of the sauce into the prepared baking dish. Cover the bottom of the dish with 4 noodles, placing them side by side. Spoon ⅓ of the mixture over the noodles. Layer 4 more noodles, ⅓ more of the mixture. Cover with the last 4 noodles and remaining mixture.

In a small bowl; stir together the butter, Parmesan and bread crumbs. Sprinkle on top of lasagna. Sprinkle parsley and paprika on top. Bake uncovered 20 to 25 minutes, until bubbly. Let cool 10 minutes before slicing.

SWEET TREATS

APPLE CRUMB BARS

Serves 6

1½ cups all-purpose **flour**
¾ cup quick-cooking **oats**
¾ cup light **brown sugar**
½ teaspoon **baking soda**
¼ teaspoon ground **nutmeg**
¾ cup cold **butter**
4 cups peeled and thinly sliced
    red **apples**
½ cup **sugar**
½ cup **water**
1 tablespoon **cornstarch**
¼ teaspoon ground **cinnamon**
½ teaspoon **vanilla extract**

Preheat your oven to 350°F.

Spray a 7 x 11-inch baking dish with nonstick cooking spray. Set aside.

In a medium bowl, combine flour, oats, brown sugar, baking soda and nutmeg, whisking well. Using a pastry blender, cut butter into flour mixture until mixture resembles coarse crumbs. Reserve ¾ cup crumb mixture for topping.

Press remainder of crumb mixture into prepared pan, pressing firmly and creating a level surface. Arrange apple slices on top of crumb base.

In a small saucepan, combine sugar, water, cornstarch and cinnamon. Bring to a boil over medium heat, whisking constantly. Cook until mixture thickens, 2 to 3 minutes. Remove from heat and add vanilla extract, whisking to blend. Pour mixture evenly over apple layer. Sprinkle reserved crumbs evenly over apple layer.

Bake until apples are tender and crumb topping is golden, 35 to 40 minutes. Let cool on a wire rack for 1 hour. Cut into bars.

RASPBERRIES ROMANOFF

Serves 4
1 cup **heavy whipping cream**
1 teaspoon **vanilla extract**
⅓ cup powdered **sugar**

3 pints ripe **raspberries**

In a medium bowl, lightly beat the cream, then add the vanilla and sugar. Whip until firm but not buttery: It should just hold peeks.

Serve in 8-ounce attractive glasses. Do a layer of berries, then cream. Repeat making 2 to 3 layers of each.

BLUEBERRY CRUNCH

Serves 6

9 cups **fresh blueberries**
⅓ cup **sugar**
⅓ cup light **brown sugar**
⅓ cup all-purpose **flour**
½ teaspoon ground **cinnamon**
¼ teaspoon ground **nutmeg**

Streusel Topping
1½ cups all-purpose **flour**
1½ cups quick-cooking **oats**
1 cup light **brown sugar**
½ cup **butter,** melted and cooled

Preheat your oven to 375°F.

Spray a 9 x 13-inch baking dish with nonstick cooking spray. Set aside.

Stir together blueberries, sugar, brown sugar, flour, cinnamon and nutmeg; toss until blueberries are coated. Spoon into prepared dish.

Streusel Topping: Combine the flour, oats and brown sugar, stir in butter. Spoon topping over berry mixture. Bake for 40 minutes or until golden.

A Note from LaDonna Rose
This is a dessert that the whole family loves. It's perfect for a hot summer day!

FRENCH COCONUT PIE

Serves **6**
4 tablespoons **butter,** melted
2 **eggs,** lightly beaten
1 tablespoon all-purpose **flour**
¾ cup **sugar**
1 cup flaked **coconut**
1 cup whole **milk**
1 (9-inch) **unbaked pie crust**
whipped cream

Preheat your oven to 350°F.

In a large bowl, combine all ingredients. Pour into pie crust. Bake until firm, about 45 to 60 minutes. Cool on wire rack. Serve with whipped cream.

HEAVENLY KEY LIME PIE

Serves 6

1 (14-ounce) can **sweetened condensed milk**
3 **egg yolks**
2 teaspoons **lime zest**
½ cup **Key lime juice**
1 (9-inch) **graham cracker pie crust**
1 cup **heavy whipping cream**
3 tablespoons **powdered sugar**
fresh **lime slices,** for garnish

Preheat your oven to 350°F.

Whisk together condensed milk and next 3 ingredients until well blended. Pour mixture into pie crust.

Bake for 15 minutes or until pie is set. Cool completely on a wire rack (about 1 hour).

Beat the cream at high speed with an electric mixer 2 to 3 minutes or until soft peaks form, gradually adding powdered sugar. Top pie with whipped cream. Chill 1 hour before serving. Garnish if desired.

A Note from LaDonna Rose
Heavenly Key Lime Pie is simple to make and really says, "I love you."

INDEX OF RECIPES

THE CLASSICS

Halibut and Chips	16,17
Halibut Ceviche	18
Halibut Chowder	20
Grilled Halibut Caesar Salad	22
Fish Tacos with Mango Salsa	24
Baked Halibut with Creamy Parmesan Topping	26
Bacon Wrapped Halibut	28

SIMPLE SUPPERS

Poor Man's Lobster	32
Halibut Noodle Bowl	33
Halibut in Parchment	34
Halibut Asiago Cakes	36
Halibut with Za'atar and Tomatoes	37
Sautéed Halibut with Fresh Avocado Salsa	38
Parmesan-Crusted Halibut	40
Roasted Halibut Cheeks in Lemon Butter Sauce	41
Seared Halibut with Marmalade Glaze	42
Hazelnut-Crusted Halibut with Apple Salsa	43

ON THE GRILL

Barbecued Halibut with Sundried Tomato-Basil Pesto	46
Grilled Haliburgers	47
Grilled Halibut with Lemon Butter Sauce	48
Grilled Halibut Kebobs	50
Grilled Halibut with Fresh Strawberry Salsa	52
Grilled Halibut with Citrus	54
Grilled Halibut Burritos	56
Spicy Halibut Burgers	57

HEARTY DISHES

Halibut Risotto Pomodoro	60
Halibut Enchiladas	61
Bacon Wrapped Halibut Bites	62
Halibut with Coconut-Curry and Bok Choy	64
Puff Pastry Halibut Pie	66
Baked Halibut with Pistachio-Date Crust	68
Halibut Shepherds Pie	69
Halibut with Tarragon Cream Sauce	70
Halibut and Brie in a Puff Pastry	72
Braised Halibut Puttanesca	74
Halibut Lasagna	75

SWEET TREATS

Apple Crumb Bars	78
Raspberries Romanoff	79
Blueberry Crunch	80
French Coconut Pie	82
Key Lime Pie	83

We'd like to thank you for buying our book. It really means the world to us and we are truly grateful. We genuinely hope this becomes your kitchen bible and you will enjoy cooking the recipes for yourself and your friends and family on a regular basis.

Best Fishes!
Ole and LaDonna Rose

Other Cookbooks by LaDonna Gundersen

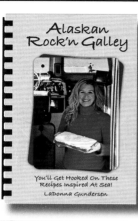

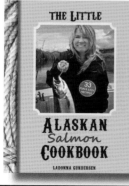

The End

NOTES